This book is dedicated to all who find Nature not an adversary to conquer and destroy, but a storehouse of infinite knowledge and experience linking man to all things past and present. They know conserving the natural environment is essential to our future well-being.

NATIONAL SEASHORES
THE STORY BEHIND THE SCENERY®
by Connie Toops

Connie Toops is a free-lance natural history writer and photographer. Her work appears in numerous conservation magazines. Previous books include *Birds of South Florida*, *The Alligator*, and *Crater Lake Trails*. Connie formerly worked as a seasonal park ranger, and her husband, Pat, is a career Park Service employee. They lived on a wilderness barrier island at Gulf Islands National Seashore for 3½ years.

Front cover: Sunrise at Cape Hatteras National Seashore, photo by David Muench; Inside front cover: Sea oats, photo by Glenn Van Nimwegen; Title page: Black skimmer chick, photo by Irene Hinke Sacilotto; Pages 2–3: Apollo Beach at Canaveral National Seashore, photo by David Muench.

Edited by Mary Lu Moore, Book Design by K. C. DenDooven

NATIONAL SEASHORES: THE STORY BEHIND THE SCENERY. © 1987 KC PUBLICATIONS, INC.
LC 87-81535. ISBN 0-88714-015-7.

"*I* *must go down to the seas again, for the call of the running tide*
Is a wild call and a clear call that cannot be denied."
—JOHN MASEFIELD

The sea is one of Nature's most captivating forces. We find ourselves drawn to it with a childlike fascination. Where land and water. meet, moods and colors change constantly. Seacoasts are dynamic environments which intensify our awareness of life itself.

Something about the seashore also appeals to our primeval senses. We are surrounded by basic elements: air, water, sand. The rhythm of the waves and the sound of the breeze lull us into tranquility. The pace of life is slow. Solitude separates us from the everyday world, and we are free to wonder at the myriad treasures the tides deposit at our feet.

The east and Gulf coasts of the United States are characterized by a shimmering chain of sandy beaches. Their landforms—the hooked arm of Cape Cod, the angular bend of the Outer Banks, the sweeping arc of Padre Island—are familiar outlines on our coastal maps. They are also pop-

ular recreation retreats. One of every four residents in the United States lives within 100 miles of these coasts.

Ten national parklands dot this shoreline: Cape Cod, Fire Island, Assateague, Cape Hatteras, Cape Lookout, Cumberland Island, Canaveral, Gulf Islands, and Padre Island National Seashores, and Gateway National Recreation Area. Each differs slightly in the character of its beaches and its native plants and animals, but all share the unique and unforgettable delights of the ocean's edge.

Breathe deeply of the salty marsh air and listen to the symphony of the surf. Savor the warm sun on your shoulders and the cool waves lapping at your toes. Lie perfectly still in the sand and watch as a curious crab tiptoes toward you or a gull soars overhead. The seashore will intrigue you with unending images of beauty and diversity.

The Dynamic Coast

The warm, sandy environments of the east and Gulf coasts may seem worlds apart from the frozen glaciers of the far north, but the creation of the seacoasts is closely linked to advances and retreats of the great ice sheets. The Ice Age, or as geologists refer to it, the Pleistocene Epoch, spanned approximately one million years. During this period world climates warmed and cooled many times. In cold eras, which lasted for thousands of years, snow accumulated in polar regions and advanced southward. Sea levels dropped as more and more water was trapped in the glacial ice. Then periods of warming set in, also lasting thousands of years. As the ice melted, seas rose, sometimes to levels higher than they are at present.

The coast is a dynamic environment. Wind and water are continually in motion. Every few seconds another wave breaks against the shore. Ocean currents carry tiny particles of sand away from some areas and deposit them in others. New spits form as old shorelines erode. From day to day and year to year, the face of the seashore changes constantly.

Thousands of years ago glaciers crushed some of the granite bedrock of eastern Canada and New England and carried the sediments to the present site of Cape Cod. Rising ocean waters lapped at the sediments when the glaciers melted. At Cape Cod, waves and longshore currents swept sand north from the beaches at Truro and Wellfleet to form the Provincelands spit.

Geologists believe the most recent advance of ice, the Wisconsin glaciation, reached its peak 15,000 to 20,000 years ago. This ice sheet originated in eastern Canada and extended across much of the northeastern United States. The snowpack was one to two miles thick, and its tremendous mass functioned like a giant bulldozer as it crunched south. Huge boulders were ground against bedrock. The resulting pebbles, clays, and sands were transported with the moving ice wall. Seas at this time were more than 300 feet below their present levels.

Let us trace the path of one granite boulder as it was crushed and ground by glacial ice. This granite was gouged from the bedrock of New Brunswick, Canada. For hundreds of years it was pushed southward, all the while being chipped and cracked as it knocked against other boulders and scouring ice. Finally it was reduced to tiny fragments of its component particles: hornblende, feldspar, mica, and quartz.

Specifically, this granite rubble was entrapped in the South Channel Lobe of the Wisconsin glacier. It had advanced to the area we know today as Cape Cod when the climate began to warm. As the glacial ice dissolved, chunks of rock and smaller sediments were swept along in swift meltwater streams. Towering mounds of this conglomerate outwash, known as moraines, were left at the terminus of the melting ice.

Concurrently in the Appalachian Mountains another geological event was taking place. Here the mountaintops were being weathered by seasonal cycles of freezing and thawing rather than by glaciers. Gigantic granite, greenstone, and quartzite boulders split from the ridgetops and tumbled onto the slopes below. Winter ice, plant acids, and probing roots gradually broke the boulders into smaller pieces. Streams of floodwater and snowmelt carried them farther down the valleys.

Eventually these rocks were reduced to quartz and other mineral components. The particles bounced along in larger streams and rivers, traversing the Piedmont and finally settling in coastal deltas. Appalachian sediments coursed down numerous watersheds in the Southeast, including the Roanoke, Neuse, Savannah, Apalachicola, and Tensaw river systems. Since ocean levels were lower during this period, the sediments were carried to deltas several miles farther out to sea than our present shoreline.

When the climate warmed once more, the Wisconsin ice melted rapidly. Water poured into the oceans and sea levels rose. What happened to

CONNIE TOOPS

Some of the sand on Fire Island is pink. Close inspection reveals red granules of garnet mixed with grains of white quartz and darker minerals. These rocks originated in upstate New York and Canada. Thousands of years ago glaciers pulverized and transported them to the coast.

that grain of granite embedded in the glacial soils of Cape Cod? Between 5,000 and 6,000 years ago, rising ocean water began to lap at the Cape's headlands. The peninsula was wider then and did not yet have the elongated sand spits which characterize it today. Storm waves crashed on shore, eroding the loose glacial fill and pulling it into the sea. There, longshore currents gained control, sweeping sand north from the beaches of Truro and Wellfleet to form the narrow, curving peninsula now known as Provincelands. Waves carried sediments from the headlands near Orleans and Chatham south to the slender Nauset and Monomony spits.

Southwest of Cape Cod another lobe of the Wisconsin glacier piled more rock rubble on eastern Long Island. As at the Cape, the sea began to erode and rearrange these sediments. Currents carried the sand westward, forming the beaches and dunes we now know as Fire Island. Today certain sections of this beach appear pink. Closer

As the climate began to warm at the end of the last glacial period, broken blocks of ice were scattered over the terrain. The ice chunks melted, leaving large craters, or "kettles." Cape Cod is dotted with small ponds where fresh water has filled these depressions.

inspection reveals red granules of garnet among the particles of white quartz sand. The garnet originated in metamorphic rocks in upstate New York and Canada. The glacier pulverized the garnet-bearing rocks as it pushed them south to Long Island. Waves and littoral, or offshore, currents then transported the grains of quartz and garnet to their present positions.

Seashores along the northeast coast are classic examples of one theory of barrier-island formation, known as "spit building." In coastal areas where sediments are abundant, as in the moraines of Cape Cod and Long Island, ocean waves erode sand, transport it downdrift, and redeposit it as narrow beach ridges. These are called spits if they are attached to land at one end. Nauset Beach on Cape Cod is a perfect example of a spit.

Fingerlike spits may eventually be overwashed by storm waves and cut off from their headlands. Once spits are separated from the mainland by inlets, they are called barrier islands. These are generally sinuous landforms that protect the lagoons, marshes, or coastal areas behind them from direct assault by ocean waves and storm surges. Fire Island, 32 miles long and less than a mile wide, is a former spit. A major storm in the late 1600s punched an opening on its western end. Two more hurricanes in the 1930s sliced an

inlet on the east, isolating the area from the rest of Long Island.

About 5,000 years ago, glacial melting slowed and sea levels stopped rising so rapidly. This period of the most recent geological events, which continues to the present, is known as the Holocene Epoch. It is within this epoch that the capes and barrier islands of the southeast coast have formed. Quartz sand and other particles transported from Appalachian watersheds to submarine coastal deltas provided the major source of building materials for all of these seashores except Padre Island. This westernmost of the Gulf barrier islands was formed by the same processes, but its sediments originated upstream in the Rio Grande, Colorado, and Brazos rivers. Since the coastal deltas were deposited when sea levels were lower, they were located several miles seaward of present river mouths. As ocean levels rose, the sediments were rearranged by waves and currents.

Waves moving toward shore carry sediments with them. The slope of the Outer Continental Shelf off the southeast coast is gentle, and waves move up this gradient in regular undulating patterns. Once a wave enters shallow water, it breaks and reforms into smaller wavelets. In breaking, it loses some of its energy and gives up a portion of

Centuries ago streams originating in the Appalachian Mountains carried tiny fragments of quartz and other minerals downstream. The sediment came to rest in deltas along the southeastern coasts, several miles farther offshore than the present barrier islands. Over the years, ocean waves moving toward shore have transported some of the sand back up the gentle slope of the Outer Continental Shelf. Underlying portions of Cumberland and other "sea islands" of the Georgia–South Carolina coast are remnants of a relic dune system that was once a mainland shoreline. Rising sea levels have inundated these older dunes and deposited new sand from the offshore deltas on their Atlantic beaches.

its sediment load. When waves of similar heights break in the same area over a long period of time, the material they drop begins to build a submerged bar. Another theory of barrier-island formation proposes that eventually enough material is dropped at the bar so that it rises above sea level. Plants can then establish themselves on the sand, and in time dunes may form. The result is a barrier island.

Proponents of a third theory believe that centuries ago sandy ridges built up along the mainland coast. The coast at that time, however, was much farther offshore. According to this theory, the edge of the former mainland has been drowned by the rising ocean. Only the higher dunes have remained above water and are now recognized as barrier islands. The low coastal plain behind them has flooded, creating the shallow lagoons that separate today's islands from the present coast.

Several barrier islands of the southeastern United States represent a combination of the preceding theories. Most of Cumberland Island, Georgia, for example, is a former dune system from the Pleistocene mainland that has been inundated by rising seas. Yet Cumberland's Atlantic beach is geologically much younger. It has been welded onto the front of the older island within the past few thousand years by sediment-laden ocean waves. All of the "sea islands" along the Georgia–South Carolina coast were formed in this manner. They are generally higher and wider than the other barrier islands of the Southeast.

Padre Island, Texas, was originally a series of submerged offshore bars. Geologists think the sand in these bars came from drowned coastal dunes belonging to an older shoreline. Several thousand years ago, wave action built the segmented bars into ridges that rose above the sea as small islands. Since then, the waves have continued to deposit sediments, finally joining the segments into a continuous island 113 miles long. Padre is the longest barrier island in the country.

SAND IN MOTION

No matter how a barrier island originally formed, it is shaped and reshaped by winds, waves, tides, and storms. The beach—the narrow strip of sand that fronts the sea—is in continual motion. Imagine that you are spending the afternoon at the shore. Spread your towel on the sand and stroll to the water's edge. All around you are patterns and landforms that tell the story of the dynamic coast.

CONNIE TOOPS

Breaking waves roll into thin, transparent sheets of water called swash. As the waves rush to shore they carry with them particles of sand, shell, and tidal debris. When the swash finally loses its forward momentum, these sediments are deposited in undulating lines on the beach berm.

A short distance offshore, breakers plunge into lathers of foaming surf. Water rushes up the beach in thin, transparent sheets of *swash*, or splashing water. Each wave carries a load of suspended sand particles. When the swash finally loses its forward momentum, the sand is dropped on the sloping foreshore. The berm crest, an elevated ridge of sand, marks the highest point on the beach that normal waves reach.

Take a few steps toward the water and you will probably notice a *scarp*—a steeply sloped drop-off a foot or so in height—where waves have scoured away some of the sand at low tide. Beyond the scarp lies the *runnel*, a submerged depression parallel to the shore. If you wade into the runnel, you will be about knee-deep in water. Beginning with this runnel, the nearshore sea bottom consists of a series of undulating mounds

and depressions. Wade out a few more paces and you may be surprised to step up onto a ridge of coarse sand. Granules eroded from the scarped beachfront and the runnel are dropped here as waves backwash into the sea. Notice also that waves coming toward shore break here. You can watch them lose some of the sediment they carry and feel it settle on your toes and the surrounding sea floor.

Seaward of the ridge lies a sandy bottom that slopes gradually from the beach. If you were to continue wading or swimming a hundred feet or more offshore, you would discover another trough that is deeper. Water here could be over your head. Immediately beyond the trough is a submerged bar. On a calm day at low tide you might be able to stand on top of it in waist-deep water. Sometimes two or three pairs of troughs

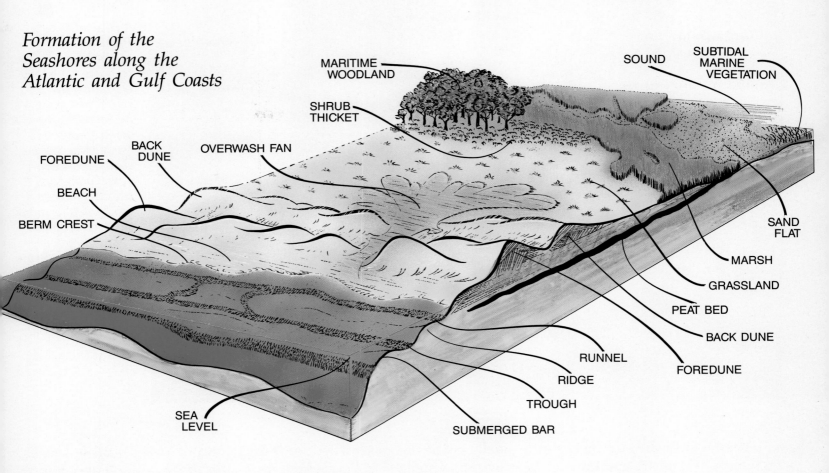

Formation of the Seashores along the Atlantic and Gulf Coasts

MARITIME WOODLAND

SHRUB THICKET

OVERWASH FAN

FOREDUNE

BACK DUNE

BEACH

BERM CREST

SOUND

SUBTIDAL MARINE VEGETATION

SAND FLAT

MARSH

GRASSLAND

PEAT BED

BACK DUNE

FOREDUNE

RUNNEL

RIDGE

TROUGH

SUBMERGED BAR

SEA LEVEL

Sand is continually reshaped by wind and water. An aerial view shows how waves breached Monomony Island at Cape Cod during a storm. Waves that overwashed the island scoured a deep inlet (right center) and moved the sand into a fan-shaped tidal delta (foreground). Such inlets are ephemeral—opening, closing, and migrating in response to ocean currents.

and bars are located off the barrier beach. Beyond them lies open ocean. During storms the bars absorb the blows of large ocean waves, dissipating part of each wave's energy before it crashes onto the barrier shore.

As you return to the beach, try a little body surfing. Catch a wave as it begins to break and allow it to wash you toward shore. The same energy that rolls you through the surf is also rolling innumerable grains of sand. They may not travel far with each wave, but consider that 8,000 to 12,000 waves come ashore each day. If a given grain of sand moved a tenth of an inch with every wave, it could migrate up to 100 feet by the end of the day!

The east and Gulf coasts experience fairly calm weather during the summer and stronger storms during the winter. Beach profiles reflect seasonal

GLENN VAN NIMWEGEN

Winter storms transform the ocean into lathers of foaming surf. Gale-force winds fling seafoam into the dunes, producing blizzardlike conditions. Huge waves slap against the shore, biting into the dunes and flattening the beach profile. Some of the sand that is eroded from the beach during winter storms is dropped at the offshore bar. During calmer summer periods this sediment will be redeposited on the beach by more gentle wave action.

Plant roots and seeds collect at the high-tide line. They are buried by windblown sand, and eventually some sprout. Pioneering species such as American beach grass and sea oats provide a windbreak, so more sand builds at their bases. Eventually dunes rise along the former drift line.

GLENN VAN NIMWEGEN

changes. In the summer, gentle swells lap at the shore. These are flat, low-energy waves that break at relatively long intervals. They pick up sand from the bars and deposit it on the foreshore, creating a wide beach with a steep berm. In winter, or during intense storms, waves are higher and strike the beach more frequently. They erode the berm and return the sand to the submerged bars. The beach becomes narrow; its berm slopes gradually. Wintertime offshore bars store sand that will build the beach again in calmer weather.

Tides are predictable fluctuations in ocean levels. The combined gravitational forces of the sun and moon pull a bulge of water through the ocean, causing these daily fluctuations. Most coastal areas experience two high and two low tides every 25 hours. At a few of the seashores, where unique shapes of local ocean basins exert their influence, only one high tide and one low tide are recorded daily. Beaches and marshes are first inundated by salt water, then drained, at regular intervals day after day. Sand and other particles are transported on tidal currents. Various plants and animals feed or become dormant during portions of these predictable cycles. Coastal life conforms to the tick of the tidal clock.

Twice each month the alignment of the sun and the moon creates a stronger-than-normal force. The resulting higher tide is called a spring tide. During spring tides or intense storms, waves spill over the berm crest and flow across the backshore of the beach. Broken plant roots, seeds,

seaweed, and driftwood carried on these surges collect where the waves disintegrate. Later, windblown sand may cover the debris. Some of the buried rhizomes begin to grow, and seeds of beach plants such as sea oats, American beach grass, or sea rocket sprout. They are fertilized by rotting algae and seaweed. Nurtured by occasional showers, some of the plants prosper.

At the seashore the wind blows much of the time. Breezes of 12 miles per hour or more are able to roll grains of sand across the beach. The harder the wind blows, the more sand it drives along. Vegetation and driftwood slow the wind, and sand builds up around these obstacles. Beach plants respond to being buried with new growth spurts. As more vegetation obstructs the wind, more sand is dropped. Eventually dunes rise along the former drift line.

Heavier grains of sediment are not transported as far on the wind. Thus the backshores of the beach and edges of the dunes accumulate materials the wind drops first. This includes shell fragments, coarse sand, and dense minerals such as ilmenite, garnet, magnetite, and tourmaline. Layers of these heavy storm-deposited minerals create dark bands in the white quartz sand. Subsequently, when the deposits are eroded by wind or waves from a new direction, striking patterns are revealed in the contrasting layers.

Some barrier islands have more and larger dunes than others. Islands that lie across prevailing winds spawn the highest dunes because sand is blown across the beaches and accumulates in the middle of the island. Shackleford Banks at Cape Lookout, for example, lies perpendicular to the fair-weather southwesterlies. It has some of the highest dunes in the region. On adjacent Core Banks the same winds blow parallel to the island, and sand cannot accumulate as readily. As a result, Core Banks is much more open and has only a few low dunes.

Unless dunes are stabilized by plants such as sea oats or beach grass, they migrate in whatever direction the wind blows. Jockey's Ridge on the Outer Banks, the Provincelands at Cape Cod, and many of the dunes on Padre Island move 35 to 75 feet per year, inundating everything in their paths. Even dunes that are held together by grasses and other beach plants continue to migrate slowly as sand blows off barren spots and into the swale behind them.

Dunes generally form in discontinuous lines with mazelike openings threading between them. When storms strike the coast, waves surge across the beach and lap at the dunes. Sometimes dunes located close to the shore are eroded. Washovers are not as destructive as they may appear, however. When dunes are breached, their sand is transported toward the back of the island. Once crashing waves enter the winding inter-dune pas-

Wind and water whisk away sand that is not securely bound by plant roots. This live oak forest is being engulfed by sand from eroding beach dunes.

JAMES A. KERN

CONNIE TOOPS

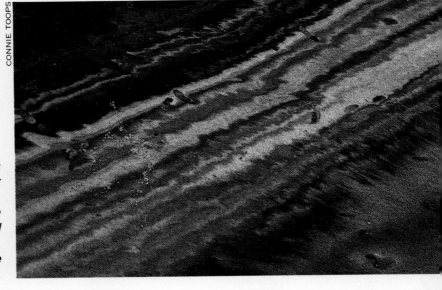

Although quartz is a common component of sand, it is not the only ingredient. Look closely and you will discover numerous dark flecks: the minerals magnetite, ilmenite, tourmaline, and garnet. These minerals are heavier than quartz, thus are dropped sooner by wind and waves. They are deposited together in black bands. Later, when wind or waves from another direction erode the sand, patterns of striking contrasts are revealed.

CONNIE TOOPS

Shallow bays and estuaries lie between the barrier islands and the mainland. When sand blows across an island, some of it drops into the quiet water along the backshore. Overwash from major storms spreads more sand into the bays. Gradually these shallows are invaded by cordgrass, rushes, and other salt-tolerant marsh plants. They stabilize the new sediments, widening the island in the direction of the mainland.

sages, they slow down. Sand eroded from the dunes is redeposited behind them in a fan-shaped layer. During severe storms sand may be swept all the way across an island, but it drops quickly into the back lagoons and salt marshes. The net effect is a redistribution of sediments from the eroded ocean beach to the widening back section of the island. Barrier beaches intercept and diffuse a significant amount of storm-wave energy before it batters the mainland.

Barrier islands are separated from the mainland by shallow sounds and bays. Sometimes storms drive huge amounts of ocean water through inlets and across low passages on islands, flooding these sounds. When the storm passes and winds shift, floodwater is forced out of the sounds in an outrush that may slice through low sections of an island. Thus a new inlet is created. Inlets allow ocean water into the bays behind the islands, providing a new source of nutrients for the myriads of marine creatures in these estuaries.

Many of these storm-created inlets are ephemeral. Each time a rising tide floods into a sound, the swiftly moving water carries sand and other sediments with it. If you watched from a vantage point above the inlet, you would notice that the flooding tide begins to lose its momentum—and its load of sand—as it enters the more quiet sound waters. Over a period of time shoals begin to build at the mouth of the sound. Ebbing tides, which drain the estuary, carry some of these sediments back to sea. Discharges from the mainland rivers that flow into the bays also flush the inlet.

But unless these currents are exceptionally strong, the shoals continue to widen.

Marsh plants invade the shoal areas, trapping more sand and eventually closing the inlet. It may take a number of years, but the original low area that was breached to form the inlet will be mended, widened, and strengthened by sand deposits and subsequent growth of marsh plants. Studies reveal that inlets have existed at one time or another in 14 different locations on Core Banks and 11 locations on Assateague Island. Usually only one or two inlets are open simultaneously on each island.

Barrier islands, and the inlets that separate them, migrate in two directions—laterally and shoreward. Waves usually strike the coast at an oblique angle rather than head-on, generating a longshore current. You may have noticed while swimming that you were carried right or left several yards from your original point of entry into the surf. You experienced longshore, or littoral, transport. Sand is moved along the shore in exactly the same way.

Littoral currents erode sand from the upstream end of an island and redeposit it farther downdrift. Older sections of a barrier island lie nearest the upcurrent end and erode first. Aged tree stumps or layers of peat formed long ago under salt marshes may be exposed in this process. If left undisturbed, littoral currents usually deposit an equivalent amount of sand on the downdrift end of the island.

At the beginning of the last century, Petit Bois Island straddled the Alabama-Mississippi state line. Since then, over seven miles of the east end have eroded, and in the associated lateral transport, nearly three miles have accreted on the west. Today the entire island lies in Mississippi. Oregon Inlet at Cape Hatteras moves in the same manner. About a mile of new sand has been deposited on the south end of Bodie Island since the inlet was widened in the Ash Wednesday Storm of 1962. The sand has been transported on the region's southward-flowing littoral current. But the inlet has not completely closed because

Sand moves from east to west along the northern Gulf coast. In the past two centuries, seven miles of the east end of Petit Bois Island (foreground) have eroded. Three miles of new shoreline have been deposited on the west end of the island. Much of the rest of the sand has been lost to a man-made ship channel dredged near the west tip.

the north end of adjacent Pea Island is slowly eroding in this same longshore transport process.

Barrier islands migrate toward shore in response to storm waves and rising sea levels. We know that when storms erode the beaches, sand is overwashed to interior sections of the island. Dunes gradually retreat from the beach as gusts of wind blow sand into the swales. Through time, storm-created inlets shoal and close, and marshes extend closer to the mainland as they invade recent sand deposits.

Storm migration may be more dramatic, but gradually rising sea levels have the same "rollover" effect on barrier islands. Geologists tell us that ocean levels are still rising slowly. Cape Hatteras and Assateague are typical of much of the coast, where the average increase is 12 inches per century. Along the northeast coast the apparent rise is less—about six inches per century—because the land there is still rebounding from glacial compression. Land along the Texas-Louisiana coast is subsiding due to removal of oil and gas and the growing mass of Mississippi River delta deposits. Subsidence, coupled with ocean-level increases, makes the apparent sea level rise here about three feet per century.

Islands respond to increasing ocean levels by slowly migrating toward the mainland. Core Banks, for instance, moves shoreward at the average rate of 1.5 feet per year. Why don't the islands eventually merge with the mainland? Rising sea levels are also inundating the coastal plain at the same rate. Land along the coast submerges at nearly the same pace that barrier islands retreat, so the distance between islands and the mainland remains fairly constant.

SUGGESTED READING

Bascom, Willard. *Waves and Beaches: The Dynamics of the Ocean Surface*. Garden City, New York: Anchor/Doubleday, 1964.

Kaye, Glen. *Cape Cod: The Story Behind the Scenery*. Las Vegas, Nevada: KC Publications, 1980.

Kaufman, Wallace, and Orrin Pilkey. *The Beaches are Moving: The Drowning of America's Shoreline*. Garden City, New York: Anchor/Doubleday, 1979.

Leatherman, Stephen P. *Barrier Island Handbook*. 2nd ed. Charlotte, North Carolina: Coastal Publications, 1982.

Leonard, Jonathan N. *Atlantic Beaches*. Alexandria, Virginia: Time-Life Books, 1972.

Life of the Shore

Despite harsh coastal conditions, certain plants and animals derive enough protection from the sun and salt spray and find enough nutrients and fresh water to thrive here. Whether at Cape Cod, Assateague Island, or Canaveral, life zones on seashores and barrier islands are similar. Beginning at the edge of the water, let us examine these habitats and the wildlife that colonizes them.

SWASH

Only a few creatures can withstand the constant pounding of the surf. Most animals of the swash zone possess either armorlike shells or the ability to burrow, drift, hop, or fly away from the impact of the breakers. Rooted plants, which would be battered by the waves, are absent.

Two of the zone's most common inhabitants, mole crabs and coquinas, allow themselves to be washed up or down the beach in the breaking waves. Streamlined mole crabs dart through the surging water to new burrows. They use shovel-like legs to dig into the substrate until only their eyes and feathery antennae extend above the sand. Mole crabs feed by straining bits of microscopic plankton from the seawater that flows past them.

Coquinas are thumbnail-sized clams that inhabit shallow beds on the shoreface. Sometimes a wave will sweep dozens of these brightly colored bivalves from their shallow burrows. As the swash drains away, each clam extends a muscular foot and pulls itself back into the sand. Like mole crabs, coquinas feed on organic debris in the water. Coquinas are commonly found on beaches from Assateague southward.

Small jumping crustaceans called beach hoppers or beach fleas scavenge the piles of seaweed and flotsam tossed ashore by the tides. They are active at night and leap erratically when disturbed. Willets, plovers, sandpipers, and gulls probe the sand and debris piles for beach hoppers and sea worms. They also patrol the break-

GLENN VAN NIMWEGEN

Sanderlings feed at the edge of the breaking waves. They patter up and down the beach, keeping just out of range of the foaming swash. They dine on mole crabs, beach hoppers, and other small invertebrates that are exposed by the surf.

Ghost crabs burrow into the sand above the high-tide line. They emerge occasionally during the daylight hours but are most active at night. They scuttle across the beach in search of dead fish and other debris washed in by the tides.

ing waves for crabs and minnows momentarily swept from deeper water. The small, drab sandpipers that zigzag along the beach at the edge of the swash are sanderlings. Someone once calculated that if we could move our legs as rapidly as they do, we could run 100 yards in five seconds!

Two of the most unusual—and eerie—of the swash zone's inhabitants can be seen only at night. Walk along in the wet sand at the edge of the water and watch for tiny bursts of blue-white light in your footprints. The animals responsible are tiny amphipods which live between the grains of sand. You may also notice luminescence in the

Coquinas, sometimes called bean clams, are dwellers of the swash zone. If incoming waves dislodge them, they quickly burrow into the sand as the water recedes. A muscular foot projects from one side of the shell; siphon tubes extend from the other. The siphons pump in food and oxygen and expel wastes.

In the south, sea oats bind the dunes with a lattice of rhizomes. The tough leaves of this grass resist salt spray, but fragile rootlets are destroyed by trampling. Caprice, a small island in the Gulf, disintegrated within a decade after its sea oats were destroyed. Visitors to seashores today are asked to remain on established trails to protect the fragile dunes.

water as waves break or fish swim by. It is caused by millions of microscopic protozoans, sometimes called "shining light-of-the-night." The effect of this shimmering greenish glow, if you are lucky enough to witness it, is unforgettable.

DUNES

Plants begin to colonize the sand at the edge of the dunes. Among the hardiest pioneers are those with leaf adaptations that enable them to survive the relentless wind and salt spray: sea rocket's repellant waxy coating, dusty miller's insulating wooly hairs, beach grass's ability to roll its leaves shut, and morning glory's ground-hugging growth form.

The dunes are bound internally by a network of plant roots. In the north the plant responsible is American beach grass. From Cape Hatteras south, the binding agent is sea oats. Both grasses send out long runners and establish new leaf clusters along each root. The roots also absorb moisture from rainfall as it percolates through the ground.

Piles of sand collect around the grasses. Instead of being buried by these windblown deposits, the grasses send out new rhizomes that grow upward. More sand is trapped; more root growth is stimulated. Eventually dunes 25 to 50 feet high are knit upon this underground network. Although beach grass and sea oats tolerate salt spray and desertlike conditions, they are destroyed by trampling. Dunes are fragile. Once their delicate root anchors give way, they are subject to rapid erosion.

When sea oats and American beach grass are buried by windblown sand, they send out underground runners. New clumps of grasses sprout from the rhizomes, trapping more sand. The sand, in turn, stimulates more runners. They trap still more sand. The dune grows, secured by an intertwined network of roots.

During the early 1920s a resort was built on the Isle of Caprice between Ship and Horn islands on the Mississippi coast. An excursion boat brought bathers and fishermen to Caprice. The island's several hundred acres of beaches also hosted a lush growth of sea oats, which the owner decided to harvest. Their pendant seed heads were then popular in dried flower arrangements. The grasses were cut and sold; the dunes were severely trampled. In 1926 a storm hit the coast. The island began to disintegrate. Sand eroded from under the dance hall, the bathhouse, and the casino. Five years later the entire development was under water. Today no trace of Caprice remains. Seashore managers now realize the importance of protecting dunes. In many areas they ask visitors not to walk or drive on them.

Half-dollar–sized holes punctuate the dunes and back beaches of seashores southward from Assateague. They mark burrows that extend two to four feet underground. The burrows belong to pale crustaceans called ghost crabs. Ghost crabs are opportunists, feeding upon dead fish, hatchling turtles, young seabirds, or picnickers' scraps. They use large, powerful claws to rip their food apart.

Ghost crabs live in the dunes, but they retain strong ties to the sea. Their gills must remain moist. When sheltered in their cool burrows, ghost crabs can survive for two days without rewetting their gills. Then they scuttle across the beach for a dip in the surf. Like their ocean-dwelling relatives, ghost crabs spawn in the sea, and their eggs hatch into free-floating larvae.

Midday dune temperatures can reach 120° F. Ghost crabs and wolf spiders, which burrow as deep as three feet into the sand, retreat to their dens. Grasshoppers and beetles climb plant stalks to escape the sweltering heat. Yet this is the environment that several species of seabirds choose for their nests. Their problem is not incubating the eggs to keep them warm but shading the eggs and chicks to keep them relatively cool.

Plovers select solitary nest sites at the edge of the dunes. Snowy plovers, rather rare and quite well camouflaged, reproduce on the Gulf Islands. Wilson's and piping plovers breed at several of the Atlantic seashores. Nests are simply sandy depressions decorated with bits of shell. Their tawny, speckled eggs blend perfectly with the background. Although tiny chicks are able to run from danger within hours after hatching, they usually crouch motionless on the sand to escape detection by predators.

American beach grass is the pioneering plant at seashores from North Carolina to New England. Like sea oats, it sends up new rhizomes when inundated by sand. After forests at Cape Cod were harvested, relentless winds began to erode the dunes. In the early 1800s beach grass was planted extensively near Provincetown to halt the dune migration. Here, it binds the sand near Old Harbor Lifesaving Station at Race Point.

JEFF GNASS

Raccoons patter through the marshes in search of crabs and shellfish and scavenge the thickets for fruits and berries. They also prey on the eggs of nesting seabirds.

IRENE HINKE SACILOTTO

A common tern offers a minnow to its chick. Least, sandwich, royal, gull-billed, and caspian terns also nest at the eastern seashores.

IRENE HINKE SACILOTTO

CONNIE TOOPS

Black skimmer chicks rest in their nest as the last egg hatches. They are superbly camouflaged to blend with the sandy background.

IRENE HINKE SACILOTTO

Horseshoe crabs lay their eggs in the sand above the tide line. Opportunistic gulls feast on exposed eggs.

Terns and black skimmers also hollow out nests in the sand at the edge of the dunes. They, however, sit in noisy, crowded colonies to raise their chicks. Terns vigorously defend their nests by dive bombing and pecking intruders. Skimmers feign a broken wing to lead potential predators away from their well-camouflaged chicks. Adult birds tirelessly fly back and forth from nests to the water, plucking up silvery minnows to feed their young. In extremely hot weather they also shake seawater from their feathers to cool the eggs and chicks.

Ghost crabs, snakes, raccoons, and feral animals feast on eggs and hatchling seabirds. Thus terns, skimmers, gulls, and pelicans frequently nest on the low, isolated "spoil" islands (built above water level by dredge deposits) adjacent to dredged channels and waterways. Here they escape many of their natural predators as well as disruption by human beach users and four-wheel-drive vehicles.

SWALE

Dunes create a barrier to wind and salt spray. In their lee, less hardy plants can gain a foothold. Swales—the open flats behind the dunes—are generally dominated by scattered clumps of beach grasses and a variety of shrubby broadleaf plants. In the Northeast, beach plum, bayberry, bearberry, and poison ivy are among the first to take hold. Many of these plants produce seeds or fruits that are attractive to songbirds, mice, voles, and deer.

Maritime gerardia adds a touch of color to the swales and salt meadows. The blossoms attract an array of butterflies, bees, and other insects.

Gnarled serviceberry trees show the effects of wind and salt spray. They may be over 100 years old, but their growth is dwarfed by the elements.

White-tailed deer roam the dunes at Fire Island.

Just as American beach grass gives way to sea oats on southern beaches, beach plum and bearberry are replaced by yaupon, wax myrtle, *Baccharis*, and goldenrod on southern swales. Where swales are periodically overwashed, as on the Outer Banks, grasses and low-growing salt-tolerant plants dominate. Otherwise, thickets of brushy vegetation crowd in behind the dunes. Rabbits, cotton rats, and mice seek shelter in these thickets from foxes and birds of prey. Rodents venture into the more open grassy fields to feed at night.

The various seashores also differ in their animal residents. Species that cannot swim or fly well may never reach islands that are separated from the mainland by large bodies of water. Deer and foxes, for example, are present on Assateague and Fire islands, both of which were attached to the mainland at one time. They are absent from

Padre Island presents an interesting contrast to the rest of the southern barrier islands. It receives only half as much annual rainfall. The resulting dry environment severely limits the growth of broad-leaved plants. Nearly 100 species of grasses, sedges, and rushes flourish on Padre, but only half a dozen shrub or tree species have been recorded. Grasslands dominate the island, with woody plants occurring only in isolated clusters.

Preceeding pages: Sunlight filters through the verdant canopy of live oaks at the southern seashores. Pendant Spanish moss dangles from the spreading branches. Resurrection ferns, mosses, and lichens cling to the furrowed bark of the trunks and larger limbs. Turkeys roost in the oaks at night. By day they strut through the shrubby understory, searching for acorns. Overhead, parula and yellow-throated warblers weave exquisite nests in the mossy draperies, and Carolina wrens fill the air with song. Photo by David Muench.

areas like Horn and Ship islands, which have always been isolated. Turtles, snakes, lizards, and other reptiles swim or cling to floating logs to reach offshore islands. But amphibians, whose moist skin is sensitive to salt and excessive drying, are not likely to survive such a crossing. Frogs and toads are not common on islands that were never attached to the mainland.

Other animals were introduced by man. Among the most famous are the Assateague ponies. Their forebears belonged to colonial settlers who grazed horses on coastal islands because no fences were required. Romantic legends

GLENN VAN NIMWEGEN

GLENN VAN NIMWEGEN

Wild horses live on Assateague, Ocracoke, and Cumberland islands and Shackleford Banks. Their ancestors were transported to the islands by early settlers. The horses were allowed to roam free, grazing on salt-marsh hay. When the settlers departed, some did not bother to round up their stock. Surplus animals from the Assateague herd are auctioned each summer by the Chincoteague Volunteer Fire Department.

indicate that some ancestral stock came from Spanish shipwrecks, but this has never been substantiated. The ponies have roamed Assateague for years, nibbling on dune grasses and salt hay. The portion of the herd that resides in Maryland is owned by the National Park Service. The Virginia animals belong to the Chincoteague Volunteer Fire Department. Each summer the Chincoteague ponies are rounded up and some of the offspring are sold at auction.

Shackleford Banks, Ocracoke, and Cumberland islands also support herds of wild horses. In addition, sheep, goats, and cattle roam free on Shackleford, while Cumberland and Horn islands are inhabited by feral hogs. All may be traced to introductions by earlier settlers. Biologists feel that some feral animals are detrimental to native wildlife. In areas where this is the case, these animals are being removed.

Several pairs of Sika deer were released on Assateague in the 1920s. These small spotted elk from Japan have reproduced steadily and now outnumber native whitetail deer more than two to one. Wildlife biologists may someday find it necessary to control the Sikas if these exotics begin to infringe on the habitat of the native deer.

MARITIME FORESTS

Once dense thickets become established, the leaves of these bushes accumulate, decay, and add humus to the soil. Taller shrubs block the wind and salt spray. Where rainfall is sufficient, trees gradually take hold. As certain trees mature, they continue to replace themselves with succeeding generations of the same species. These maritime forests represent the climax stage of each seashore's vegetation.

Maritime forests are characterized by a ragged, wind-pruned appearance. Trees are gnarled and twisted; branches that rise above the canopy are quickly tattered by gales and salt spray. The forest ceiling is low and very dense. Individual trees may be 200 years old or more, though their growth appears stunted. On the mainland the same species would be twice or three times the size, but nutrients here are scarce.

The Pilgrims discovered rich beech and oak forests on Cape Cod, but the virgin timber was soon cut for homes, ships, and fuel. Once denuded of cover, Cape Cod's dunes began to shift, and what little soil had accumulated was lost. Today where parkland replaces abandoned pastures and harvested woodlands, a new sequence

Pitch pine and cranberry are pioneer species, later replaced by beech, oak, and cedar.

of succession has begun. Pitch pine and scrubby bear oak grow on the disturbed land. In many areas they will be replaced by black oak, white oak, and beech. Wetlands now support a new generation of Atlantic white cedar, red maple, and black gum.

On Fire Island and Sandy Hook, pitch pine, red cedar, and beach plum are among the pioneering trees and shrubs. American holly, black cherry, serviceberry, and sassafras germinate under their protective cover. Although they grow slowly, they are exceptionally salt tolerant and sturdy. Some of the hollies may live up to 300 years. Shade on the forest floor is too dense to support many understory plants, but greenbriar, wild grape, and Virginia creeper vines dangle just below the canopy. Box turtles occasionally lumber through the leaf litter. Searching for toads, mice, or bird eggs, black racers wind their way over and around branches.

At Assateague the forest is guarded by a tangle of wax myrtle, bayberry, red maple, and holly. Greenbriar, muscadine grape, and poison ivy vines bind the shrubs together. Past this imposing barrier, on sandy secondary dunes near the bay, grow towering loblolly pines. Beneath their cathedral-like roof lies a carpet of pine needles and a blanket of cool, still air. Whitetail and Sika deer browse at the edge of the thicket. At Chincoteague National Wildlife Refuge endangered Delmarva fox squirrels scamper from limb to limb gathering pine nuts. Mosquitoes and biting flies invade the forests during some seasons.

Loblolly pine seedlings do not grow well in their own dense shade. Under thick cover, holly, sassafras, and southern red oak seem to be gaining a foothold. But the pines are much more resistant to salt spray, storm overwash, and fires than are the hardwoods. Wherever such disturbances open a window in the canopy, young loblolly seedlings quickly sprout and prosper. On Assateague these pines may represent the pinnacle of succession, the "storm climax."

The Outer Banks are low and overwashed frequently, so grasses predominate. Myrtle and red cedar thickets grow up in the lee of some dunes. Only in a few places—such as at Nags Head, Buxton, and Shackleford Banks—are the islands high and wide enough to support true maritime forests. Loblolly pine, American hornbeam, bay, holly, and dogwood grow in these forests, but live oak, a southern species, dominates. Gnarled live oak branches are encrusted with lichens. Gray squirrels feast on abundant seeds and acorns, and songbirds flock to the sheltering woodlands.

Tangles of thorny greenbriar, grape, and poison ivy form imposing thickets at the edges of many maritime forests. Songbirds seek refuge in the dense cover, and the berries provide food for birds and small mammals.

Freshwater ponds support a lush growth of willows, cattails, and grasses. Muskrats and raccoons live here year-round. Teal and other waterfowl are seasonal visitors. Turtles bask in sunny spots along the shore, and dragonflies zip through the air in pursuit of deerflies and mosquitoes.

DAVID MUENCH

In the moist depressions between the forested ridges, lenses of fresh water surface. Here cattails, ferns, and duckweed grow.

Classic examples of live oak forests flourish at Cumberland Island and the Florida Gulf Islands. The Deer Point Naval Live Oaks Reservation was set aside in 1827 as America's first tree farm, a precursor of the national forest idea. Live oaks were especially valuable then as compass timbers (lumber with natural curves that could be shaped into angular timbers) in wooden sailing ships. These oaks were planted, cultivated, and harvested at Deer Point for that purpose until the mid-1800s. Today the forest at Gulf Islands preserves a new generation of these magnificent trees.

The oak forests at Cumberland Island and the Florids Gulf Islands grow on sandy ridges where decaying organic matter has enriched the soil.

Live-oak forests grow on the sandy ridges of Cumberland Island and the Florida Gulf Islands. The sturdy, angular oaks were once prized for their lumber, which was harvested for ship timbers.

JAMES A. KERN

Cabbage palms and mangroves, both tropical species, typify the wetlands of Canaveral National Seashore. Manatees frequent the warm, quiet backwaters of Mosquito Lagoon and Indian River.

Compared to other zones, this is a fertile and protected niche. It is also a visual feast of greens. Sunlight penetrates in occasional filtered shafts through the verdant oak canopy. Draperies of slaty Spanish moss hang limp in the humid air. After a shower douses the forest, resurrection ferns, which cling to the furrowed trunks of larger trees, unfurl glossy emerald leaves. Jade-colored mosses and lichens decorate upper branches of oak trees.

Beneath the oaks, parrot-green palmetto fronds carpet the forest floor. Where sunlight strikes them, pointed palmetto leaves are haloed in translucent gold. Carolina wrens and cardinals flit about in the shady understory. On Cumberland they are joined by flocks of wild turkeys, which dine on acorns and roost at night in the thick oak canopy.

At Canaveral live oaks grow on hammocks, or tree islands. Quite a few of these are located on old Indian shell mounds. Many tropical species reach their northern limit of growth in these hammocks: mastic, wild coffee, marlberry, torchwood, and stopper. Branches of these trees are festooned with bromeliads, which resemble pineapple plants, and shoestring and serpent ferns. There are even a few species of orchids; they are epiphytes—subtropical plants that cling to the bark and upper branches of host trees. They de-

rive their nutrients from sunlight, rainfall, and decaying plant material that accumulates in their cupped leafstalks. Gopher tortoises and indigo snakes, both endangered, also live amidst the hammocks.

Other parts of Canaveral, Cumberland, and the Gulf Islands are dominated by pines: loblolly, longleaf, slash, sand, and pond. Usually these stands of pine are the result of fires or storm-caused disturbances. Palmetto, scrub oak, and yaupon form a matted growth of shrubs in the understory. Armadillos, rabbits, raccoons, king snakes, and several species of woodpeckers are frequent visitors to the pinelands.

Yaupon thickets cover the backsides of the dunes at southern seashores. The wind-pruned canopy provides shelter for numerous songbirds, mice, and rabbits.

30

PONDS

Pools and ponds dot the seashores. Some form on the beaches where spits close off small embayments. Others originate where blowouts between dunes erode to the level of the water table. Winding sloughs (slews), which are fed by tidal creeks, bisect several of the southern islands. Kettle ponds, created where huge blocks of glacial ice rested centuries ago, are common at Cape Cod. Salinities in these ponds vary from fresh to brackish, but almost all of these watering holes support a variety of life.

At the edge of the water, dragonflies and frogs rest on cattails or rushes. Small turtles bask in the sun. Herons and egrets stalk the minnows that dart among reedy tussocks. Alligators cruise the waters of the southern seashores. Raccoons patter about in search of aquatic prey. Muskrats, a few otters, and mink also inhabit some of the ponds. Rafts of ducks and coots are common during migration. Of all the coastal life zones, ponds and maritime forests provide the most stability and diversity.

Frogs, toads, and salamanders have porous skin that is sensitive to salt water. These amphibians are more numerous where seashores were attached to the mainland than on isolated barrier islands.

Ponds form in depressions between the dunes. Water lilies survive seasonal water fluctuations by floating on the surface. Maples, gums, and oaks grow in profusion where their roots can sink into the water-saturated earth.

Salt Marshes

Salt marshes are much more uniform than ponds, and much more fertile. Each acre of marsh produces more edible plant material than any domestic crop except sugar cane. Salt marshes occupy the landward edges of barrier islands and fill in the banks of coastal creeks. As sand is washed across the island or built up on flood-tide deltas, it is colonized by a thick growth of salt-marsh cordgrass. This hardy plant, which grows along coasts from Canada to Texas, thrives where it is inundated by daily tides. Higher marshland, flooded only during storms or spring tides, is carpeted with mats of salt hay, salt-marsh spike grass, black needle rush, or blackgrass.

Marshes buffer the wave action of adjacent lagoons, so silt settles out between the cordgrass clumps. Dying leaves fall into the muck. In time a layer of peat forms. Fiddler crabs, whose burrows line the tidal creek banks, venture into the grasses as the tide falls. They dine on decaying bits of plant material known as detritus. Periwinkle snails glide along the grass blades and across the muck, rasping off tiny particles of food.

Raccoons, rails, herons, egrets, gulls and shorebirds descend on the marsh at low tide to devour snails, crabs, and the ribbed mussels that lie half buried in the peat. Nutrients from detritus, cycled through this marsh food chain, are eventually returned to the water and washed into the winding creeks. Here crabs, shrimp, and juvenile forms of many sport fish grow. The salt marsh is not as inviting as many of the coast's other habitats. The odor of decomposing detritus is repulsive to some, the mucky substrate is nearly impossible to walk through, and salt-marsh mos-

Vast expanses of salt marsh line the landward edges of the seashores. Tidal creeks wind through the marshes, providing a haven for blue and fiddler crabs, oysters, clams, and the young of many sport fishes. Cordgrasses, sedges, and rushes grow in profusion on the mucky substrate. Saltwort, a multi-branched succulent plant, grows on sandier ground. It turns ruby red in the autumn.

quitoes are usually abundant. Yet salt marshes are extremely important to all sorts of wildlife.

During certain seasons mosquitoes do seem to rule the marshes, but only female mosquitoes bite humans. They ingest blood in order to lay eggs. Eggs hatch into larval wigglers, which develop in the water about two weeks before they molt and fly. Adults live up to six months. Despite the nuisance they create for us, mosquitoes are an important food source for fish, dragonflies, bats, swallows, nighthawks, and several species of ducks. Mosquitoes both see and smell their victims. By wearing light-colored clothing and avoiding use of perfumes and scented soaps when hiking in mosquito country, we can escape some bites.

The Surrounding Sea

A nutrient-rich detritus soup flows from the salt marshes into the bays and sounds. These lagoons are nurseries for creatures of the sea. Over two thirds of all the fishes in the Gulf and the Atlantic depend upon estuaries during some period of their lives. Just as grasses bind the dunes and carpet the marshes, underwater grasses play an important role in estuarine life cycles.

Eelgrass, recognized by its long, tapelike leaves, grows on sandy bay bottoms along much of the Atlantic coast. A whole community lives in the shelter it provides: encrusting algae, sea squirts, shrimp, clams, scallops, crabs, snails, and a host of fishes. Over two dozen species of waterfowl eat its seeds and roots. Widgeongrass, a pondweed that grows on muddier bay bottoms, is also very attractive to the flocks of geese, ducks, and swans that migrate through or overwinter at the seashores.

Along the southern coasts, tropical pondweeds—shoalgrass, turtle grass, and manateegrass—are more common. Over 300 species of marine animals live among these sea grasses. A floating plant, sargassum, forms a similar community. This tangled brown algae, commonly called seaweed, originated in the Sargasso Sea near the Tropic of Cancer. Large mats of sargassum drift in the ocean, providing food and pro-

IRENE HINKE SACILOTTO

Large flocks of snow geese winter on the ponds and estuaries of the eastern shore. Among their favorite foods is widgeon grass, a narrow-leaved pondweed. When ponds are frozen, geese search for grains such as wild rice.

tection for tiny barnacles, shrimp, crabs, snails, and fishes. Sometimes storms toss sizable chunks of sargassum and other seaweeds on the beach.

Bays, sounds, and lagoons are mixing pots. Fresh water enters at the mouths of mainland rivers. Seawater rolls through inlets with the tides. Normally, fresh water floats on heavier salt water, but tides, waves, and temperature gradients cause some mixing. Nearer the barrier islands, water is generally more saline. Shrimp, crabs, and many species of fishes spawn in the ocean or near barrier islands. Once their eggs hatch, the tiny offspring drift into the estuaries. They feed there on free-floating microscopic plants and animals called plankton. Some seek submerged grass beds; others enter salt-marsh creeks. Finally, as they grow and mature, they return to the open sea.

A young black-crowned night heron peers from its hiding place in thick marsh vegetation.

IRENE HINKE SACILOTTO

GLENN VAN NIMWEGEN

Mute swans are native to the Old World. They have been imported for ponds in formal gardens and city parks. Escapees nest in coastal marshes from Massachusetts to Virginia.

IRENE HINKE SACILOTTO

Fiesty snapping turtles inhabit fresh and brackish ponds.

Tricolored herons wade through shallow tidal creeks in search of minnows.

Horseshoe crabs lay their eggs during the highest spring tides.

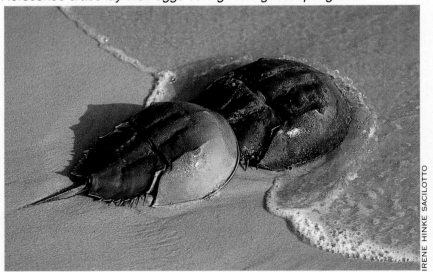

IRENE HINKE SACILOTTO

IRENE HINKE SACILOTTO

IRENE HINKE SACILOTTO

Waterfowl crowd the refuges during the winter. Pintails prefer shallow bays and marshes, where they feed on aquatic vegetation. When startled, they rise quickly from the water.

Monomony, Jamaica Bay, Chincoteague, Pea Island, Cedar Island, and Merritt Island—all wildlife refuges adjacent to the national seashores—are excellent places to watch coastal animals. Ducks, geese, swans, ospreys, herons, and shorebirds nest or feed near the lagoons. Bays and sounds teem with aquatic life.

The meandering creeks and tidal marshes at Chincoteague NWR, Virginia, provide excellent habitat for waterfowl and wading birds.

PAT TOOPS

Sand dollars live offshore in shallow sand. Their delicate shells are sometimes found washed up on the beach.

Blue crabs host barnacles, which ride piggyback on their shells.

CONNIE TOOPS

DAVID MUENCH

Bay bottoms and offshore sands are the homes of numerous marine worms, anemones, mollusks, sea stars, and urchins. Many of these creatures are seen by beachcombers when their shells or remains are cast upon the shore. Some of the most common shells on the east and Gulf coast seashores include: whelks, moon snails, slippers, arks, scallops, sea pens, sand dollars, starfish, and horseshoe crabs.

Watchful beachcombers may also be rewarded with glimpses of the large mammals that inhabit offshore waters. Bottlenose dolphins, known for their playful riding of boats' bow waves, are the most abundant marine mammals along the southern coasts. Individuals or small groups regularly feed on schools of mullet, menhaden, or shrimp near shore. In cooler northern seas the Atlantic white-sided dolphin is more common. It is wary of a close approach to boats, but it can be recognized at a distance by a white band on each side and its short black beak.

Only 10,000 or so humpback whales remain in the world's oceans. One group feeds at a fishing bank north of Cape Cod during the spring, summer, and fall. Every winter the animals migrate to the Caribbean. During migration, sightings are sometimes reported from Fire Island and the Outer Banks. Fin whales are also occasionally seen from or found stranded on these beaches. Endangered right whales, reduced by whaling to a population of approximately 200 worldwide, are observed seasonally in Cape Cod Bay. This bay is also a frequent site for strandings of pilot whales. Scientists are still unable to explain why pods of these animals beach themselves *en masse* and die.

Harbor seals winter as far south as Assateague. On sunny winter days they may be seen hauled out on quiet stretches of beach at Cape Cod and Fire Island. Manatees, or sea cows, prefer more tropical waters. They feed in the mangrove-lined estuaries of Mosquito Lagoon and Indian River at Canaveral. During the summer they range north to Cumberland Island and have been seen at Gulf Islands.

Summer beachwalkers from Cape Hatteras to Padre Island may encounter bulldozerlike tracks in the sand. They identify a spot where a sea turtle, probably a loggerhead, has come ashore to lay eggs. Only female sea turtles venture onto land, and then only to nest. Eggs incubate about two months in the warm sand before the infant turtles hatch and scramble back to the sea.

Many suitable nesting beaches have been destroyed over the years, making the active turtle

CONNIE TOOPS

Bulldozerlike tracks identify the crawl of a female loggerhead turtle. These huge animals spend most of their life at sea but return to beaches on the southeast coast early in the summer to nest. Sea turtle populations have declined drastically in recent years. Turtles were hunted extensively for food, leather, and jewelry. Nesting beaches have been developed. Countless turtles drown when they become entangled in fishing nets.

Rangers mark sea turtle nests and return in about two months to check whether the eggs have hatched. Sometimes the nests are overwashed with new sand, making it difficult for the babies to dig their way out. Rangers rescue the trapped turtles and release them near the shore.

CONNIE TOOPS

nests at southern seashores all the more significant. Baby turtles are easily confused, since they hatch at night. Instinctively they head for areas of brighter light. If artificial lights overpower the illumination reflected from the ocean, the hatchlings end up wandering hopelessly on the beach or dunes, falling victim to raccoons, ghost crabs, and other predators.

Despite a high reproduction rate, few hatchlings reach adulthood. If they do, their troubles are not over, because larger turtles are often caught and drowned in shrimp nets. Loggerheads are presently listed as a threatened species. The other Atlantic and Gulf sea turtles—green, leatherback, hawksbill, and Kemp's ridley—are all endangered.

Only 2,000 Kemp's ridley sea turtles survive today. In 1947 a 16-mile stretch of Mexican beach supported 40,000 ridley nests. Twenty years later only 700 nests were located. This Mexican beach is the ridley's only known nesting site. Scientists at Padre Island are now hatching some of the eggs collected in Mexico on the park's beaches. It is hoped that the babies will imprint (recall the specific location where they hatched) on the Texas sand and return to Padre Island to nest in the future.

Rangers at the southern seashores conduct special patrols during turtle nesting season. Loggerhead nests are fairly common at Canaveral, Cumberland, and Cape Lookout. Rangers mark the nests and relocate eggs laid in high-hazard areas. As hatching time approaches, they monitor the nests closely. If the babies are unable to dig free of the sand by themselves, rangers rescue them and release them into the sea. These special turtle projects are examples of the stewardship we must exhibit toward creatures of the sea if we wish to see them survive.

SUGGESTED READING

CROSLAND, PATRICK D. *The Outer Banks.* Arlington, Va: Interpretive Publications, 1981.

National Park Service, Division of Publications. *Assateague Island.* Handbook 106, Washington, D.C.: U.S. Government Printing Office, 1980.

THOM, VALERIE. *Cumberland Island: A Place Apart.* National Park Service, Washington, D.C.: U.S. Government Printing Office, 1977.

WEISE, BONNIE R., and WILLIAM A. WHITE. *Padre Island National Seashore: A Guide to the Geology, Natural Environments, and History of a Texas Barrier Island.* University of Texas, Bureau of Economic Geology, Guidebook 17. Austin: University of Texas Press, 1980.

WHITMAN, DAVID, and others. *A Place Apart: Canaveral National Seashore.* Philadelphia, Pa.: Eastern Acorn Press, 1987.

Man and the Seashores

Because the coast changes so rapidly, few archaeological sites remain to tell us about the prehistoric Indians who used these seashores. Historians believe most were nomadic groups who hunted game and harvested fish and shellfish. They probably traveled to the islands in dugout canoes. Middens of oyster and clam shells in some of the coastal parks attest to the Indians' heavy dependence upon seafood.

Various mariners explored the coast within a few years of Christopher Columbus's epic journey. Spaniards searched for gold and a passage to India along the Gulf coast in the early 1500s. They found neither. In 1559 Don Tristán de Luna brought a group of colonists to Pensacola Bay. They labored for two years raising cattle and crops before a hurricane dashed their hopes. Other Spanish and French Explorers tried to establish outposts near Padre Island and the Gulf Islands, but none succeeded until the early 1700s.

Sir Walter Raleigh organized the first English settlement in the New World. He sent two ships of explorers to the Virginia Colony in 1584. The following year, over a hundred soldiers and adventurers landed on Roanoke Island, North Carolina, and remained through the winter. Then supplies ran short, and parleys with the Indians turned sour. The settlers scurried back to England.

Raleigh recruited more colonists—among them this time 17 women and 9 children—and sent them back to the "Cittie of Ralegh" under the governorship of John White. They reached Roanoke Island in July 1587. A month later White's daughter gave birth to Virginia Dare, the first English child born in North America.

White returned to England for more supplies, leaving the colonists to their tasks of gardening and building houses. A war with Spain prevented his return for three years. By then the entire colony had disappeared. The only hint of its fate was the word "Croatoan" carved on a post of the pallisade wall. Although no trace of the settlers was found, historians surmise that they were attacked by Indians. Either the colonists were killed, or they were absorbed into the tribes.

In November 1620 the *Mayflower*, carrying 101 Pilgrims from England, nearly ran aground on Cape Cod's shoals. These religious settlers had hoped to reside further south, but with winter fast approaching, they accepted the shelter of Cape Cod Bay. Although more than half died during that winter, the survivors were befriended by local Indians who taught them to hunt, fish, and grow corn. Within 20 years of the Pilgrims' arrival, other colonists established several new towns on Cape Cod.

IRENE HINKE SACILOTTO

No trip to the seashore would be complete without an exhilarating romp in the surf.

Completed in 1870, Cape Hatteras light towers 180 feet above the beach. It warns sailors of Diamond Shoals, the "graveyard of the Atlantic."

In the late 1830s three brick light towers were built on the Nauset bluffs. They marked Cape Cod's dangerous outer bar until 1892, when erosion toppled them into the sea. The "three sisters" were temporarily replaced by triple wooden light towers. In 1923 the present iron lighthouse was erected. It exhibits an alternating red and white beacon at night.

The following century witnessed more settlement along the coasts. Colonists grazed cattle, sheep, and hogs on salt hay. They raised corn, beans, pumpkins, and tobacco. Drift whales, which sometimes stranded on the beaches, were rendered into profitable oil. Later, colonists learned to build deepwater whaling ships and pursued these valuable animals on the high seas. Giant trees from the maritime forests were harvested for ship timbers, lumber, and firewood. Settlers realized they could evaporate seawater to produce salt, and salt could be used to preserve seafood. Fishing grew from a part-time to a full-time profession. Fleets of sailing ships plied the coastal waters for cod, halibut, mackerel, and shellfish.

Other residents earned a living piloting ships through treacherous shoals or lightering the freight of large vessels into smaller boats that served inland waters. Citrus growing was the main occupation near Canaveral. Padre Island supported a huge cattle ranch. Market hunting—the mass slaughter of shore birds and waterfowl—and egg collecting were profitable for a while. But within a few years bird populations, especially at Cape Cod, Assateague, and along the New Jersey shore, were severely reduced. The natural resources of the seashores were being heavily tapped.

Early coastal villages were linked by water routes rather than roads. As trade expanded, shipwrecks became more common. Frugal colonists salvaged whatever they could: cargoes of bananas, sugar, molasses, rum, preserved meat, bricks, lumber, precious metals, and even the ships' fittings and timbers. Merchants and shipowners, however, could not sustain large-scale losses of cargo and ships, so they began to establish privately operated navigational aids and shelter huts for shipwrecked seamen near the most dangerous shoals and inlets.

The oldest functioning lighthouse, a privately built structure, stands at the gateway to New York City. This nine-story octagonal light first warned sailors of the shifting channel near Sandy Hook in 1764. It has remained in continuous service since then. Other hazardous points were illuminated over the years: Cape Cod (Highland) in 1787, Cape Hatteras in 1802, Cape Lookout in 1812, and Fire Island in 1827. As more lighthouses appeared along the coast, a system to regulate them was needed. In 1789 the U.S. Lighthouse Service assumed this responsibility. Smaller lights were added to mark harbors and inlets. Older structures were gradually modernized or replaced. By the 1870s the east and Gulf coasts were reliably lit for mariners.

Early lighthouses depended upon candlelight, magnified by lenses, to create a navigational beam. Later, oil lamps replaced candles. Sandy Hook light was originally illuminated by 48 whale-oil burners. In 1822 French physicist Augustin Fresnel invented a system of prisms and lenses that created a single powerful light beam. His design is still in use today in some lighthouses. Fresnel lenses were rated in six orders. First-order lenses

The Ocracoke lighthouse was completed in 1823 and has remained in continuous operation since then. It is the oldest functioning lighthouse on the Outer Banks.

DAVID MUENCH

CONNIE TOOPS

The Sandy Hook light was first illuminated in 1764. The 103-foot tower is the oldest working lighthouse in the nation. Its third-order white light, visible about 19 miles offshore, is magnified by a Fresnel lens installed in 1857.

were used in the most prominent seacoast lights; sixth-order lenses were installed in harbors. The Highland, Fire Island, Bodie Island, Cape Hatteras, and Cape Lookout lighthouses all exhibited first-order lights.

Lightkeepers and their families lived at the isolated stations. Every day the keeper climbed the winding stairs to polish the lens and the storm windows, trim the wick, and replenish the oil. He was responsible for maintaining the beam from dusk until dawn. The job was both lonely and hazardous. In 1874 the Brazos Santiago light tower at the south end of Padre Island collapsed during a hurricane and killed the keeper's wife. Another hurricane smashed the Horn Island light in 1906, drowning the keeper, his wife, and their daughter. In 1939 the Coast Guard assumed all

lightkeeping duties. Lights are now electric, and many operate on automatic timers.

A few years after the first lighthouses illuminated the coast, the Massachusetts Humane Society began building lifesaving huts on remote beaches. They were stocked with food and blankets to sustain shipwrecked sailors who reached shore alive. Years later the U.S. Congress authorized a few coastal lifeboat stations, the first of which was built on Sandy Hook in 1848. By 1871 the U.S. Life-Saving Service operated a network of these stations.

Life stations were built three to eight miles apart along most of the coast. Each was staffed by a keeper and six surfmen. Every night from late summer through the following spring they patrolled the beaches. The night was divided into

A small bronze cannon, developed in 1878 by Captain D. A. Lyle of the Life-Saving Service, was used to fire a line to a ship in distress. The Chicamacomico Lifesaving Station was constructed on the Outer Banks in 1874 and remained in service for 80 years. From it and other similar coastal stations, surfmen carried out thousands of daring rescues of ships wrecked in the treacherous shoals.

ARLINE ZATZ

DAVID MUENCH

three watches. During each, one man walked to his left and another to his right until they met the surfman from the adjacent station. They exchanged tokens as proof of the meeting, then returned. All the while they scanned the breakers for any signs of vessels in distress.

If a sinking vessel was sighted, the surfman signaled to it with a flare, then rushed to the station to summon the rest of the crew. Depending upon the situation, the keeper would either order out the surfboat or the mortar cart—a wagon that carried ropes and hoisting equipment. Initially, few stations had horses, so the surfmen dragged the heavy carts through the sand.

When the seas permitted use of the surfboat, the men rowed through the breakers to the capsized vessel. They usually had to make several exhausting trips to rescue all the passengers and the crew. Occasionally they even salvaged some of the cargo. If the seas were too rough for the boat, a Lyle gun was employed. The Lyle gun was a small cannon used to fire a line to the ship. It is the only gun ever invented to *save* lives. Once the line was in place, hawsers were stretched between the ship and the beach, and the stranded seamen were hauled off one at a time in a breeches buoy. Women and children could be transported in a similar manner in watertight life cars. The Life-Saving Service later merged with the Coast Guard, and today helicopters replace the surfmen's feats of daring. In their era, however, the men of the Life-Saving Service performed some of the most heroic acts ever witnessed along the coasts.

COASTAL DEFENSE

The War of 1812 proved the vulnerability of our nation's coastline. Military leaders immediately began planning a chain of nearly 700 fortifications to protect strategic harbors and shipping channels from Maine to Texas. Forts would be located close enough to the water to bombard enemy fleets and prevent naval blockades.

As part of this coastal defense plan, a star-shaped granite fort was begun on Sandy Hook in the mid-1800s. Technological improvements in cannons, however, made the masonry fort obsolete before it was completed. Major renovations at the post, including installation of concrete bunkers for powerful mortar and gun batteries, were completed in the 1890s. Although used until after

PAT TOOPS

Fifteen-inch Rodman smoothbore cannons were mounted at many seacoast forts. They could fire a 15-inch 300-pound cannonball a distance of three miles.

CONNIE TOOPS

Today visitors at Gulf Islands and Gateway NRA may tour forts and gun batteries that span over a century of military presence on the coasts.

World War II, the officers' quarters, barracks, and guardhouse of today's Fort Hancock look much as they did at the turn of the century. Fort Tilden, across the bay at Breezy Point, also guarded New York harbor.

Pensacola'a navy yard and deep harbor were defended by forts at three strategic points: Santa Rosa Island, Perdido Key, and the mainland bluffs. Enemy ships entering the harbor would be trapped in a deadly crossfire. Fort Barancas, built against the hillside on the site of a former Spanish battery, had a commanding view of the water. Huge Fort Pickens, designed to garrison 600 troops and over 200 cannons, actually saw more duty as a prison than a battleground. As at Sandy Hook, concrete batteries and long-range artillery replaced the aging masonry forts. On Santa Rosa Island today, visitors can inspect military installations dating from 1828 to World War II.

Ship Island's deep harbor and proximity to New Orleans made a perfect site for Fort Massachusetts. Its construction began in 1859.

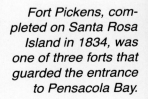

CONNIE TOOPS

Fort Pickens, completed on Santa Rosa Island in 1834, was one of three forts that guarded the entrance to Pensacola Bay.

"Morning brought with it a twenty-seven mile [per hour] gale," remembered Orville Wright. "Nobody imagined we would attempt a flight in such weather." But fly they did—for a wavering twelve seconds over the sands of Kitty Hawk, North Carolina. Today a monument marks the spot where their dreams were fulfilled.

HIGH FLIGHT

Orville and Wilbur Wright, bicycle makers from Dayton, Ohio, became obsessed with the dream of flight. They searched for a suitable test site—open land with soft sand, no trees, and steady wind—and chose an area south of Kitty Hawk, North Carolina. Each autumn from 1900 through 1902 they brought their gliders to the dunes and tested aerodynamic principles. In 1903 they returned with another fragile craft, this one equipped with a small gasoline engine. On their first attempt in this plane on December 17, they flew 120 feet. Their dream of flight was realized!

Aviation history is linked to the east coast. Floyd Bennett Field, now part of Gateway National Recreation Area, was the first municipal airport in New York. Wiley Post used it as a base for his record-setting solo flight around the world, and other famous aviators, including Howard Hughes and John Glenn, frequented the field. In 1962 the National Aeronautics and Space Administration (NASA) began developing a space center on Merritt Island. Hundreds of satellites and interplanetary probes have been launched from the center, adjacent to Canaveral National Seashore. Manned space flights, moon explorations, and Space Shuttle flights have become almost routine. In less than a century the Wright Brothers' dreams have blossomed beyond their wildest imaginations.

SUGGESTED READING

CIPRA, DAVID L. *Lighthouses and Lightships of the Northern Gulf of Mexico.* New Orleans: U.S. Coast Guard Public Affairs Office, 1976.

MERRYMAN, J. H. *The United States Life-Saving Service,* 1880. Golden, Colorado: Outbooks, 1981.

ROBINSON, WILLARD B. *American Forts: Architectural Form and Function.* Chicago: University of Illinois Press, 1977.

STICK, DAVID. *Dare County: A History.* Raleigh: North Carolina Department of Cultural Resources, 1970.

———. *North Carolina Lighthouses.* Raleigh: North Carolina Department of Cultural Resources, 1980.

Captain Edward Penniman, a whaler, built a lavish Second French Empire–style home at Cape Cod.

RETREAT AND RECREATION

Seashores have traditionally been the sites of residences and vacation retreats for those who could afford the shore's isolated grandeur. Nearly two hundred years ago Phineas and Catherine Greene Miller built an elegant mansion on Cumberland Island. They lived in the refined style of southern planters, while slaves toiled in the surrounding fields to raise cotton. A hundred years later Lucy Carnegie, widow of the steel magnate, financed another Cumberland Island mansion called Dungeness. Subsequently, four more mansions, including one with its own golf course, were built for the Carnegie children. Plum Orchard, one of these elegant homes, now is being restored by the Park Service. On Cape Cod, well-to-do sea captain and whaler Edward Penniman also lived in luxury. His home remains as an example of the architectural excellence of the period.

Jamaica Bay, part of Gateway NRA, lies at the doorstep of New York City. Thousands of ducks and geese rest at the refuge during migration. In spring the marshes teem with nesting waterfowl and songbirds.

At Great Kills on Staten Island, a peat bog merges with the shorelines of Raritan and Lower New York bays. Many city children have their first opportunity to go swimming and beachcombing here.

45

IRENE HINKE SACILOTTO

On the coasts, moods and colors change constantly. The rich scenery and abundant wildlife provide ample opportunities for photography.

For years coastal islands were relativ isolated. New bridges and causewa however, made them targets development. Today a chain of natio seashores, recreation areas, a wildlife refuges protects the natu wonders of the east and Gulf coas

CONNIE TOOPS

One of every four U.S. residents lives within 100 miles of a coast, making seashores popular destinations for vacations and weekend camping trips.

Nags Head was famous some years ago as a summer resort for the rich. More recently, wealthy investors have erected exclusive beach homes on Fire Island.

Until a few decades ago, however, most of the outer Banks remained undeveloped. These low islands were subject to frequent storm overwash and were considered unsafe for permanent structures. Then, as part of a 1930s public works project, the CCC fortified dunes on Hatteras, Pea, and Bodie islands with fencing and planted them with beach grasses and shrubs. The immediate result was higher and seemingly more stable dunes. Investors felt safer. Homes and hotels were constructed close to shore. A highway was built across the islands.

Over the years residents learned that the higher dunes do not allow natural overwash. Sand no longer sweeps across the islands to widen their backsides. Beaches still erode on the ocean side, so the islands become narrower. When storm waves breach the dunes, a wall of water inundates homes and resorts near the sea.

Sandbagging, groins, and beach nourishment projects have been attempted to control beach erosion. Over $20 million has been spent at Hatteras, but none of these projects have succeeded. They have actually accelerated erosion in certain areas. When the Cape Hatteras light was built in 1870, it stood well back from the sea. Today, even

Clamming is a favorite seashore pastime. Succulent quahogs and razor clams are easiest to harvest at low tide by searching for "keyholes." These are shallow depressions where clams' siphons have been withdrawn through the mud. The slitlike holes indicate where the clams are buried.

IRENE HINKE SACILOTTO

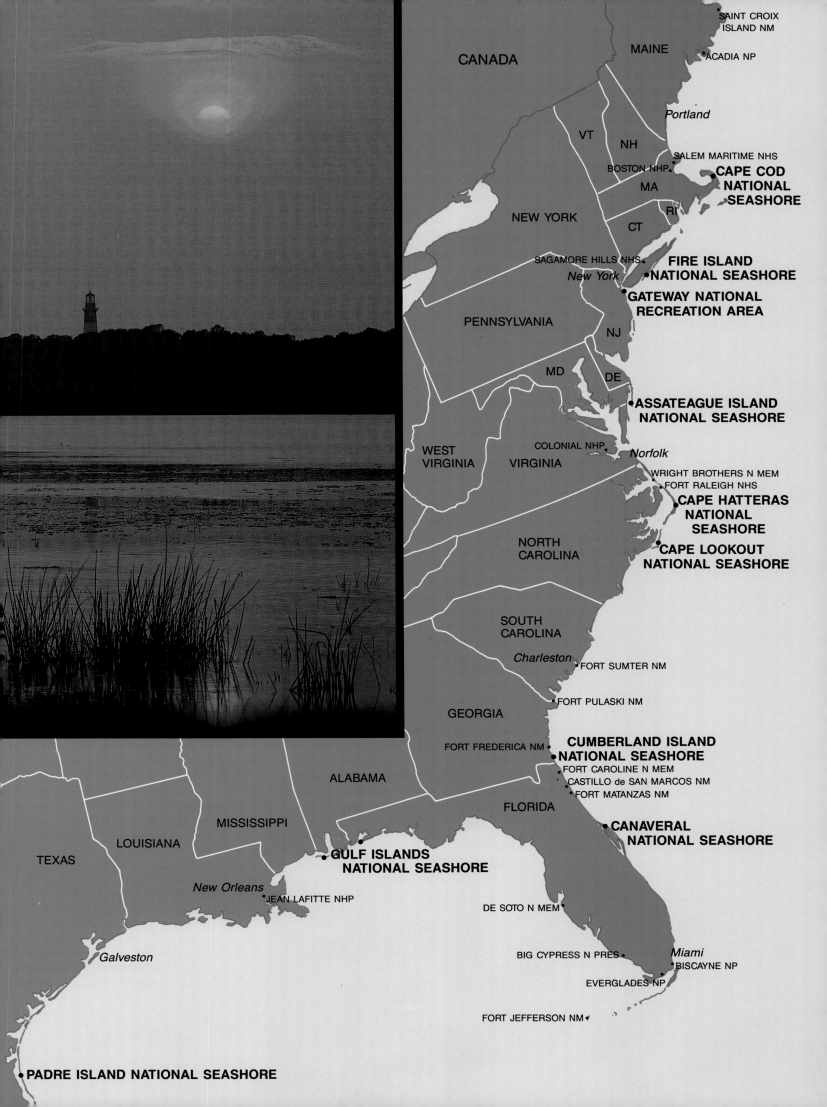

SAINT CROIX
ISLAND NM

CANADA

MAINE

ACADIA NP

Portland

VT

NH

SALEM MARITIME NHS

BOSTON NHP

**CAPE COD
NATIONAL
SEASHORE**

MA

RI

NEW YORK

CT

SAGAMORE HILLS NHS

**FIRE ISLAND
NATIONAL SEASHORE**

New York

**GATEWAY NATIONAL
RECREATION AREA**

PENNSYLVANIA

NJ

MD

DE

**ASSATEAGUE ISLAND
NATIONAL SEASHORE**

WEST
VIRGINIA

COLONIAL NHP

VIRGINIA

Norfolk

WRIGHT BROTHERS N MEM

FORT RALEIGH NHS

**CAPE HATTERAS
NATIONAL
SEASHORE**

NORTH
CAROLINA

**CAPE LOOKOUT
NATIONAL SEASHORE**

SOUTH
CAROLINA

Charleston

FORT SUMTER NM

FORT PULASKI NM

GEORGIA

FORT FREDERICA NM

**CUMBERLAND ISLAND
NATIONAL SEASHORE**

FORT CAROLINE N MEM

CASTILLO de SAN MARCOS NM

FORT MATANZAS NM

FLORIDA

**CANAVERAL
NATIONAL SEASHORE**

ALABAMA

MISSISSIPPI

LOUISIANA

**GULF ISLANDS
NATIONAL SEASHORE**

TEXAS

New Orleans

JEAN LAFITTE NHP

DE SOTO N MEM

Galveston

BIG CYPRESS N PRES

Miami

BISCAYNE NP

EVERGLADES NP

FORT JEFFERSON NM

PADRE ISLAND NATIONAL SEASHORE

after stabilization, it is only a few hundred yards from the water's edge.

Cape Hatteras and Cape Lookout provide an interesting comparison. Both belong to the same island chain. Habitat at Cape Hatteras has been manipulated; Cape Lookout has been left in a fairly natural state. Overwash and island migration continue normally at Cape Lookout. Few developments touch the islands, so storms are not great causes for concern. The beaches remain wide. Cape Lookout light, built in a situation similar to the one at Cape Hatteras, is in no danger from the sea.

By the early 1960s quite a few of the seashores and coastal islands had been linked by bridge or causeway to the mainland. Promoters eagerly eyed the long stretches of beach. Fortunately Congress believed that everyone, not just the wealthy, needs access to the sea. Taking a cue from Cape Hatteras, which became a national sea-

shore in 1953, Congress authorized the National Park Service to add eight more seashores and a recreation area during the period from 1961 to 1975.

Also learning from the Outer Banks, seashore managers are wary of overdeveloping these delicate coasts. They realize the shores are subject to hurricanes and winter storms. One of a barrier island's most important functions is to buffer the energy of storm waves before it assaults the mainland. This is best accomplished if the island remains in as natural a state as possible.

So the seashores exist for all to enjoy. They present timeless images: squawking gulls, warm sun, shimmering water, curious treasures of the sea. The shore is a fascinating environment, one of dynamic natural processes and of far-ranging moods and contrasts. Seashores provide discoveries to renew our curiosity and refreshment to restore our soul. And they exert an almost mystical power to draw us back time and time again.

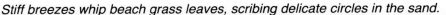

Stiff breezes whip beach grass leaves, scribing delicate circles in the sand.

GLENN VAN NIMWEGEN

Inside back cover: Grasslands cover most of Padre Island, but one small clump of live oaks remains. Photo by David Muench

Back cover: A diamond-patterned lighthouse, completed in 1859, marks Cape Lookout. Photo by David Muench

Books in this series: Acadia, Alcatraz Island, Arches, Blue Ridge Parkway, Bryce Canyon, Canyon de Chelly, Cape Cod, Capitol Reef, Channel Islands, Civil War Parks, Crater Lake, Death Valley, Denali, Dinosaur, Everglades, Fort Clatsop, Gettysburg, Glen Canyon–Lake Powell, Grand Canyon, Grand Teton, Great Smoky Mountains, Haleakala, Hawaii Volcanoes, Lake Mead–Hoover Dam, Lincoln Parks, Mount Rainier, Mount Rushmore, Mount St. Helens, National Park Service, National Seashores, Olympic, Petrified Forest, Rocky Mountain, Sequoia–Kings Canyon, Scotty's Castle, Shenandoah, Theodore Roosevelt, Virgin Islands, Yellowstone, Yosemite, Zion

Published by KC Publications · Box 14883 · Las Vegas, NV 89114

Printed by Dong-A Printing Co., Ltd., Seoul, Korea
Separations by Kwangyangsa Co., Ltd.
Typography by Stanley Stillion